WITHDRAWN

LIBYA
...in Pictures

Prepared by
Geography Department

Lerner Publications Company
Minneapolis

VISUAL GEOGRAPHY SERIES®

Publisher
Harry Jonas Lerner
Senior Editor
Mary M. Rodgers
Editors
Lori Ann Coleman
Joan Freese
Colleen Sexton
Photo Researcher
Beth Johnson
Consultants/Contributors
Tom Streissguth
Abdi Samatar
Sandra K. Davis
Designer
Jim Simondet
Cartographer
Carol F. Barrett
Indexer
Sylvia Timian
Production Manager
Gary J. Hansen

Photo by Dick Bancroft

A group of children shares a joke outside a school in Tripoli, Libya.

This book is a newly commissioned title in the Visual Geography Series. The text is set in 10/12 Century Textbook.

LIBRARY OF CONGRESS CATALOGING-IN-PUBLICATION DATA

Libya in pictures / prepared by Geography Department, Lerner Publications Company.
    p. cm.—(Visual Geography Series)
    Includes index.
    Summary: Examines the topography, history, society, economy, and government of Libya.
    ISBN 0–8225–1907–0 (lib. bdg.)
    1. Libya. [1. Libya.] I. Lerner Publications Company. Geography Dept. II. Series: Visual geography series (Minneapolis, Minn.)
DT215.L535   1996
961.2—dc20   95–39567

International Standard Book Number: 0–8225–1907–0
Library of Congress Catalog Card Number: 95–39567

Photo by Dick Bancroft

Many Arab men in Libya still wear a traditional cloth head-piece, which historically helped to keep blowing sand out of the clothes and faces of desert travelers.

Acknowledgments

Title page photo © Betty Crowell.

Elevation contours adapted from *The Times Atlas of the World,* seventh comprehensive edition (New York: Times Books, 1985).

1 2 3 4 5 6 – JR – 01 00 99 98 97 96

Tripoli, the capital of Libya, features an interesting mix of new and old architecture.

Contents

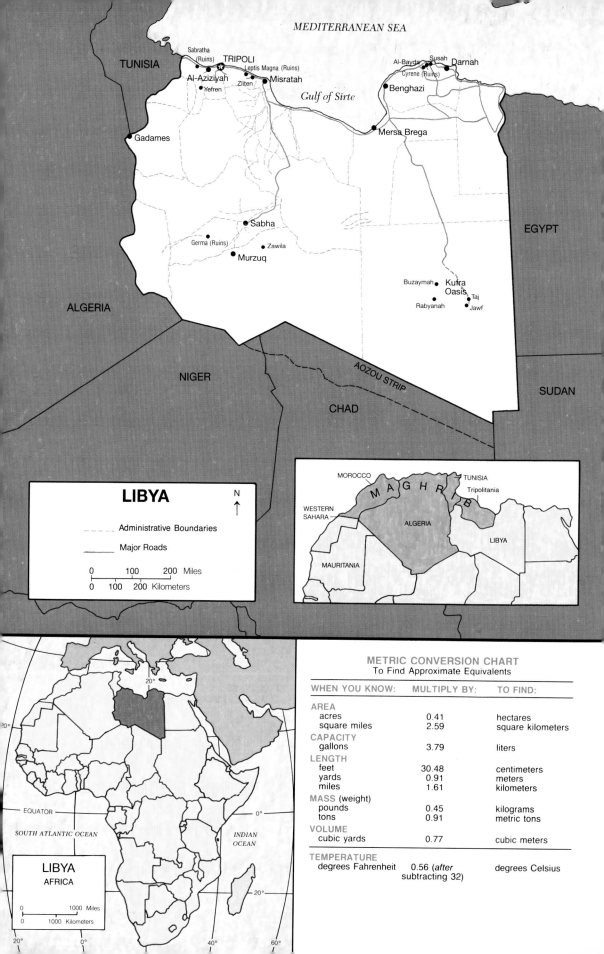

MEDITERRANEAN SEA

TUNISIA

Sabratha (Ruins)
TRIPOLI
Leptis Magna (Ruins)
Al-Aziziyah
Zliten
Misratah
Yefren

Gulf of Sirte

Al-Bayda
Susah
Darnah
Cyrene (Ruins)
Benghazi

Gadames

Mersa Brega

EGYPT

ALGERIA

Sabha

Germa (Ruins)
Zawila
Murzuq

Buzaymah
Kufra Oasis
Rabyanah
Taj
Jawf

NIGER

AOZOU STRIP

SUDAN

CHAD

LIBYA

N ↑

--- Administrative Boundaries

— Major Roads

0   100   200 Miles
0   100   200 Kilometers

MOROCCO
TUNISIA
M A G H R B
Tripolitania
WESTERN SAHARA
ALGERIA
LIBYA
MAURITANIA

LIBYA
AFRICA

EQUATOR
20°
20°
0°
SOUTH ATLANTIC OCEAN
INDIAN OCEAN
20°
40°
60°

0   1000 Miles
0   1000 Kilometers

METRIC CONVERSION CHART
To Find Approximate Equivalents

WHEN YOU KNOW:	MULTIPLY BY:	TO FIND:
AREA		
acres	0.41	hectares
square miles	2.59	square kilometers
CAPACITY		
gallons	3.79	liters
LENGTH		
feet	30.48	centimeters
yards	0.91	meters
miles	1.61	kilometers
MASS (weight)		
pounds	0.45	kilograms
tons	0.91	metric tons
VOLUME		
cubic yards	0.77	cubic meters
TEMPERATURE		
degrees Fahrenheit	0.56 (*after* subtracting 32)	degrees Celsius

A passerby walks along the wall that surrounds Gadames, an oasis community near Libya's border with Algeria and Tunisia. Oases—fertile areas with water supplies—dot the Libyan Sahara.

Introduction

The fourth largest nation on the African continent, Libya lies in North Africa. Until the twentieth century, Libya was the name of the general area and not of a unified nation. Yet this sparsely populated land has since gained the world's attention for its rapid economic growth as well as for political controversy and conflict.

Libya has long been a crossroads, linking three continents. For centuries people have met in Libya on their way to and from the Middle East region to the east, Europe across the Mediterranean Sea to the north, and the rest of Africa beyond the vast Sahara Desert to the south.

Nomadic hunters were the first inhabitants of Libya. Ancestors of the Berbers were among the earliest peoples, followed by conquerors and colonists from ancient Phoenicia, Greece, and Rome. Bringing

Tall Roman columns loom over the ruins of Leptis Magna, an ancient Roman city that flourished near Tripoli. Libya was part of the Roman Empire for several centuries.

Photo by Dick Bancroft

their new faith of Islam, Arabs from the Middle East came to North Africa in the seventh and eighth centuries A.D., followed by Bedouin clans from what is now Saudi Arabia. By the late 1500s, the Ottoman Turks ruled Libya, whose Mediterranean harbors became major centers of trade and piracy. The Ottomans controlled the Libyan ports and earned huge sums by trading central Africa's gold, ivory, and other goods to wealthy Europeans.

In the nineteenth century, several European nations founded colonies in Africa, hoping to control the continent's valuable trade routes and natural resources. As the Ottoman Empire declined, the southern European nation of Italy sent settlers and military forces to Libya to establish an Italian colony. But to maintain its hold on the region, Italy fought a fierce guerrilla war against the Libyans, who sought freedom from foreign rule. After Italy's defeat in World War II (1939–1945), the future of Libya was decided by the United Nations (UN), an international diplomatic organization. By a vote of UN members in 1951,

Libya became an independent monarchy, with King Idris I as its first ruler.

Libya has undergone enormous change since it became a self-governing nation. In 1959 engineers discovered huge underground deposits of oil in Libya's deserts. The export of oil made Libya a wealthy nation, able to invest in new industries and to provide better education, health care, and social services to its people. Ten years after the discovery of oil, a young army colonel named Muammar el-Qaddafi overthrew King Idris. Qaddafi's revolution transformed Libya from a monarchy into a strict socialist nation. The government owns major resources and industries, allows only one political party, and carefully controls the economy as well as the media.

Qaddafi's lifelong goal has been to unify the Arab states of the Middle East and North Africa into a single socialist nation. But this dream has brought political and military conflict to Libya. Some African countries accuse Qaddafi of supporting revolutionaries and terrorists who seek to overthrow the governments of Libya's neighbors. Bombings and other acts of terrorism have been linked to Qaddafi's government. As a result, Libya has faced military attacks from the United States and harsh criticism from some UN members.

The UN has banned some forms of international trade with Libya. In the mid-1990s, the UN also threatened a boycott of Libyan oil exports—an action that would devastate the Libyan economy. Although Libyans are enjoying the prosperity brought by oil wealth, they also are suffering from isolation within the global community.

Muammar el-Qaddafi *(center)*, **the head of the Libyan government, meets with other national leaders to discuss international affairs. Over the years, policies pursued by Qaddafi have lost him the support of many countries.**

A whitewashed mosque stands out among the earth-colored buildings of an oasis in Libya's Sahara Desert.

1) The Land

Libya is a nation of far-reaching arid lands in north central Africa. From the shores of the Mediterranean Sea, the country extends southward into the vast Sahara Desert. More than 90 percent of Libyans make their homes in northern cities and towns near the seacoast. The rest of the population lives in scattered villages and desert oases—isolated areas of fertile soil and freshwater springs. The country's land area totals 679,216 square miles, making Libya about twice the size of the state of Alaska.

Libya at its widest point stretches 1,050 miles. From the coast to the country's southernmost point is 930 miles. Moving clockwise Libya's neighbors are Egypt to the east, Sudan, Chad, Niger, Algeria, and Tunisia.

Topography

Libya has two major geographic regions—the Mediterranean coastal lowlands and the Sahara Desert. Along the country's western Mediterranean coast are sandy beaches, salt marshes, and shallow lagoons. Tripoli, Libya's capital, lies on this part of the coast. Near the border with Tunisia is the Gefara Plain, an area that supports hardy shrubs and grasses. An important farming zone, the plain spreads southward to the Jabal Nafusah, a long limestone ridge that runs from west to east and reaches an elevation of 2,500 feet above sea level.

In eastern Libya, the Plain of Marj parallels the Mediterranean coast, which juts northward and then eastward toward Egypt. Forests of pine and juniper trees cover the 3,000-foot Jabal al-Akhdar, or Green Mountain, to the south of the coastal plain. Farther south, stony, tree-covered hills and plateaus give way to the Sahara Desert.

The western and eastern strips of coastland are home to most Libyans. A narrow section of desert called the Sirte separates the two coasts, extending northward to the Gulf of Sirte and blending

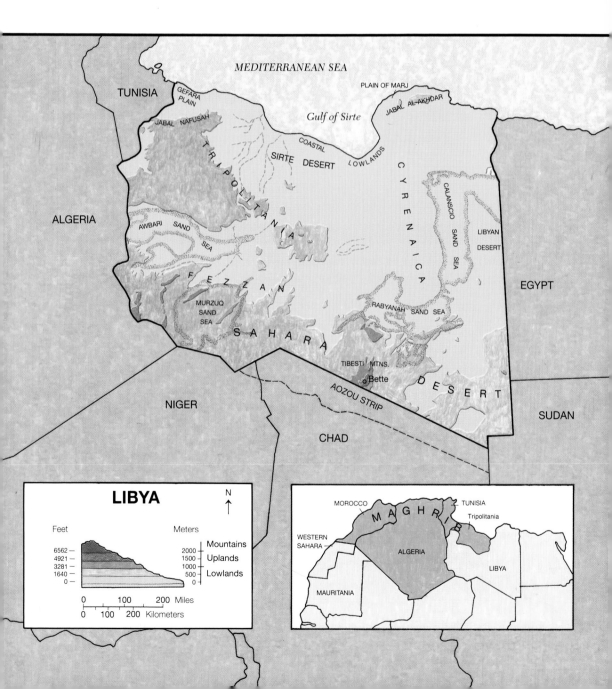

Photo by Dick Bancroft

Long stretches of the Libyan coastline lack an abundance of natural vegetation, offering instead sandy beaches, salt marshes, and in some areas groves of olive and date palm trees.

southward into the Sahara. In many places, only salt marshes and oil pipelines mark the landscape of the Sirte, which has long been a barrier to travel and commu-nication between Libya's western and east-ern ends of the Mediterranean coast.

South of the coastal lowlands sprawls the enormous Sahara Desert, which cov-

Photo © Bernard Regent/The Hutchison Library

The town of Yefren lies in the Jabal Nafusah, a mountainous plateau southwest of Tripoli. The Jabal Nafusah marks the end of Libya's coastal plain and the beginning of the Sahara Desert.

Oil pipelines stretch across the desert in southeastern Libya. Besides the pipelines and oil wells, few signs of human activity appear in this part of the Sahara.

ers more than one-third of Africa. One of the driest areas on earth, the Sahara was once a well-watered grassland teeming with game and human activity. But climatic changes thousands of years ago turned the region into a sea of gravel and sand, where vast, waterless plateaus lie among mountains of black volcanic rock. Oases dot some parts of the Sahara. In these spots, wells have been built to extract water from deep beneath the sand, allowing people to form communities and grow crops or raise livestock.

The Sahara can be divided into many different sections. In western Libya, the Sahara Desert is mostly uninhabited except for scattered oases. Sabha and Murzuq, two of the largest oases in this area, support nomadic herders as well as settled farmers. These two oases stand between two vast expanses of sand dunes—the Awbari Sand Sea to the northwest and the Murzuq Sand Sea to the south. Wide, rocky highlands spread across much of the rest of the western Libyan Sahara.

The Calanscio Sand Sea and the Rabyanah Sand Sea in southeastern Libya include thousands of square miles of tall sand dunes that constantly shift like waves and travel with the desert's prevailing winds. The Tibesti Mountains cross the southern Libyan border into Chad and include Bette (7,400 feet), Libya's highest point.

The Libyan Desert is a vast, barren plain within the Sahara that lies along the country's southeastern borders with Egypt and Sudan. Few trails or settlements exist in this wilderness, parts of which were not explored by outsiders until the early twentieth century. Most of the region's population is centered in the Kufra Oasis—an area made up of several settlements, including Jawf, Taj, Rabyanah, and Buzaymah.

Climate

Throughout Libya the climate is dry and hot. In the north, however, steady southern breezes from the Mediterranean Sea help moderate temperatures throughout the year. The coastal city of Tripoli averages 52° F in January, the coldest month, and 90° F in July, the hottest month. But high temperatures in Tripoli and in other Libyan cities often break 110° F. The highest temperature ever recorded on earth,

11

Snow can sometimes fall at high elevations in northern Libya. These mountainous regions receive the most precipitation in the country.

137.7° F, scorched Al-Aziziyah, a town near Tripoli, in 1922.

Libyan winters usher in cooler temperatures to the country's mountains, where the soil often freezes. Cold, wet winter air sometimes brings light snow to the plains and highlands of northeastern Libya, a region that receives up to 20 inches of precipitation each year. In fact, the Jabal al-Akhdar is the wettest part of Libya, with as much as 24 inches of annual rainfall. Benghazi and Tripoli, the country's two largest cities, each average 14 inches of precipitation a year. Violent storms sometimes strike the coast in winter and spring.

In the Sahara Desert, temperatures vary greatly from day to night. The daytime sun reflects off the barren ground, radiating heat just above the surface. The lack of cloud cover, which would help retain the heat, causes nighttime temperatures to fall drastically. Thermometer readings in the Sahara often break 100° F at midday and then plunge to below freezing at night.

The clouds that form over the highlands of northern Libya usually drop their precipitation before reaching the desert. As a result, most places in the Sahara get less than four inches of rain a year, and some villages and oases see no rain for years at a time. The oasis of Sabha, one of the driest towns on earth, receives an average of 0.4 inches of rainfall each year. The valleys of the Tibesti Mountains in the south receive slightly more precipitation than the surrounding desert, allowing for some grazing.

Every five or six years, northern Libya suffers a severe drought that destroys crops and dries up water wells. Another danger is a dry, hot wind known as the ghibli, which often passes northward across the desert in the spring and summer. The ghibli's blinding sandstorms kill crops and livestock with a sudden dramatic temperature rise of 30 to 40° F.

Water Resources

A lack of dependable rainfall has made water an extremely important natural resource throughout Libya. The country has no permanent rivers and no freshwater lakes. Water found in the marshes and depressions near the seacoast is too salty for drinking or for irrigation. The streams in the northern highlands run only during rainy seasons. During storms dry streambeds known as wadis sometimes fill and overflow, causing sudden floods that can damage crops and buildings.

The development of agriculture has worsened the country's water problems. Irrigation projects that draw water for crops from underground aquifers (water reserves) have depleted the wells that many towns rely on for drinking water. In addition, when aquifers run low, the remaining water comes into contact with natural salts in the sand and rocks through which the water passes. This process can leave the water too salty for drinking or for crops.

In an attempt to accumulate more water for farms in the north, the Libyan government began the Great Man-Made River project in 1984. This system of pumps, canals, and reservoirs links desert wells to coastal farming regions, allowing farmers in the north to raise crops on once-barren

Independent Picture Service

Libya's cultivated fields benefit from extensive irrigation systems, which help farmers grow crops but use up large amounts of water.

land. But the Great Man-Made River also threatens the livelihood of the desert's nomadic herders, who need the wells to provide water for themselves and their livestock.

Flora and Fauna

Despite its harsh climate, Libya supports a wide variety of wildlife and vegetation that has adapted to life in the desert. In some highlands of the Sahara, wild olive and cypress trees—some of them thousands of years old—survive on sparsely watered hillsides. Esparto grass, once a principal export, is still gathered for its tough fiber, which is made into rope. Date palms grow in coastal cities and in oases, providing a staple food as well as fiber and building material.

Many varieties of cacti, including the edible prickly pear, thrive throughout the country. Lilies, narcissus, and lotus flowers bloom in the valleys of the Jabal al-Akhdar, where underground streams also water tough juniper and cypress trees. Since the 1950s, Libya has carried out several forestation programs, planting millions of eucalyptus, acacia, cypress, and cedar trees in the highlands and plains of the north. The goal of these programs has been to provide Libyans with their own lumber supply.

Foxes, hyenas, wildcats, and jackals live in parts of the Sahara. Nomads and travelers in the desert often spot gazelles and a small, horned antelope known as the addax. Lizards and snakes survive in the hottest regions by burrowing underneath the sand during the day and hunting at night when the temperature drops. Libyan desert dwellers watch carefully for scorpions and poisonous snakes such as the adder.

A well-known desert rodent, the jerboa, uses its long legs to leap over sand and gravel in the Sahara. The jerboa is a favorite prey of hawks and eagles that nest

In many parts of northern Libya where natural vegetation has been depleted, people have planted grasses in a gridlike pattern to prevent erosion and to keep the desert from creeping farther northward.

Photo by Archive Photos

Photo © Michele Burgess

A golden jackal scans the arid landscape. Jackals in North Africa generally inhabit areas with enough moisture to support trees and bushes, which provide shelter and food for the animals' prey.

Photo © Michele Burgess

The fennec, or desert fox, lives in dry areas in Libya and throughout North Africa. Fennecs have extremely large ears, which work like radars to help the animals locate the small rodents they hunt for food.

in the dry highlands of the south. Vultures also fly over the desert, while gulls, terns, and ducks favor the salty marshes of the coastal regions.

Natural Resources

Libya was long a poor nation that could do little to develop its natural resources. The discovery of oil in the 1950s had a dramatic effect on the Libyan economy and society. Foreign companies rushed to the Sahara to conduct further explorations. The Libyan government used some of the income from oil exports to make massive new investments in cities, transportation systems, and social programs.

Libyan crude oil is lighter than most other oils, making it easier to handle and less expensive to ship overseas. The oil's low sulfur content also allows it to burn more cleanly, causing less air pollution. In the 1990s, new oil explorations continue, mostly in northwestern Libya and in the seafloor off the coast.

The country also has deposits of iron ore—an important ingredient of steel—as well as potash, coal, gypsum, and manganese. Sea salt is gathered from the lagoons and depressions along the Mediterranean coast. Natron, a hardened form of salt, is collected for use in oil refining, soap making, and water purification. Limestone, granite, and marble quarries supply the country's busy construction industry.

Cities

Libya's main cities cluster near the Mediterranean coast, where most of the country's agriculture and industry also are concentrated. More than 70 percent of Libya's 5.2 million people live in urban areas. Tripoli, the largest city in the country, lies on the western part of Libya's coastline. Benghazi, the nation's second largest city, is across the Sirte Desert on the eastern shore.

Since the discovery of oil in Libya in the 1950s, Tripoli has become a bustling urban center, with modern buildings, wide roads, and the inevitable traffic jams.

TRIPOLI

Libya's capital since 1951, Tripoli has about one million residents—one-fifth of the country's population. The capital is also Libya's busiest port and main manufacturing and transportation center.

Tripoli's harbor has been an important center of trade for nearly 3,000 years. The Phoenicians—a people from the Middle East—first settled the site, which they called Oea, in the eighth century B.C. When the region fell under Roman control in the first century B.C., Oea became the seat of a wealthy and fertile province that provided huge shipments of grain to the Roman Empire. Tripoli later became the destination of well-traveled caravan routes that linked the coast with trading centers far to the south beyond the Sahara.

Under Ottoman rule from the sixteenth through the nineteenth centuries, Tripoli's harbor sheltered pirates who menaced Mediterranean shipping and dealt in stolen goods and hostages. Italian architects and engineers expanded the city in the early twentieth century, adding wide boulevards, office buildings, parks, small factories, and new apartment complexes. During the oil boom of the 1960s and 1970s, new high-rises and factories appeared on the city's outskirts as thousands of newcomers arrived from the countryside to find work in industry.

At the center of Tripoli is a medina, an old section with narrow, winding streets. Here people crowd the suqs, or open-air markets, where many sorts of foods, spices, clothing, and other goods are sold. Small, neighborhood mosques (Islamic houses of worship) in this part of the city are open for prayer each day.

Tripoli's major industries include oil refining, textile manufacturing, food processing, and the making of handicrafts such as carpets and leather work. Each year the city hosts the Tripoli International Fair, an exhibition of manufactured goods and handicrafts. The city also is home to the National Archaeological Museum, which exhibits artifacts from Libya's ancient civilizations. The museum is located in the city's Red Castle, the seat of Ottoman and, later, Italian rule in Libya.

SECONDARY CITIES

Benghazi (population 400,000) is the nation's second largest city and the main port and urban center of northeastern Libya. Lying along the shores of the Gulf of Sirte, Benghazi is a center for oil production and

Although Tripoli has become a contemporary city, historical monuments and other old sections of town remain important elements of the capital's identity.

refining. Benghazi's busy port also hosts cargo ships that bring foreign imports, including food, machinery, and raw materials, to Libya.

The ancient Greeks founded the port of Euhesperides on the site of what is now Benghazi in the 630s B.C. Later, under Turkish rule, the city was the administrative center of the Ottoman pashalik (province) of Cyrenaica. The city changed hands several times during World War II (1939–1945), when German, Italian, and British forces fought fierce desert battles for control of Cyrenaica. Benghazi became the seat of Libya's first university in 1955.

Misratah (population 100,000), on the western coast of the Gulf of Sirte, is Libya's third largest city. The historic center of the town was once a gathering point for caravans that had traveled across the Sahara Desert from central Africa. In the twentieth century, Misratah has become the hub of Libya's carpet industry.

Sabha, the largest Saharan oasis in Libya, claims a permanent population of 18,000. The community grew rapidly during the economic spurt of the 1950s and 1960s, when new schools, hospitals, roads, and an airport were built. For the first time, irrigation canals in the surrounding desert brought a reliable source of fresh water, which attracted a more permanent population.

An ancient center of Libya's caravan trade, Sabha marks an important junction of two major trails linking the Mediterranean coast to the interior of Africa. Some caravans still move between Sabha and other isolated oases of southern Libya, where camels provide the most dependable means of transportation on the unpaved routes that cut through the hot, dry desert.

Photo by Archive Photos

The Jazeer Hotel is one of several accommodations catering to visitors in Benghazi, a city on the Mediterranean coast in northeastern Libya. Because the city suffered extensive damage during World War II (1939–1945), nearly all the present-day buildings were constructed after the war.

A large number of ancient rock paintings in southeastern Libya help scientists determine how people lived and what their environment was like thousands of years ago. The earliest paintings, which feature mostly symbols and human figures, were created around 8000 B.C. Later pictures illustrate daily life, wild and domestic animals, and chariots. By about 500 B.C., the paintings began to include writing.

2) History and Government

People have inhabited Libya since at least 8000 B.C. At that time, a mild climate and fertile soil allowed farmers to raise livestock and crops in the plains and mountain valleys. Nomads moved across a well-watered savanna (grassland) in the south, where they tracked and hunted large herds of lions, giraffes, elephants, and antelope.

Over the centuries, many different peoples crossed Libya in search of cropland and fertile pasture for their herds. One such group called itself the Imazighan, or "free people." The Imazighan arrived from southwestern Asia sometime after 3000 B.C. They spoke many different dialects and had no central authority or government. Organized in extended family groups and tribes, they gradually spread across and occupied all of northern Africa.

At the same time, northern Africa was undergoing a drastic climate change. Rainfall decreased, and the topsoil of the region gradually turned to infertile sand. No longer able to grow crops, those who had been farmers became nomadic herders.

They traveled in search of water and grazing land for their herds of sheep and goats. Some nomads rode horses and horse-drawn chariots and began trading goods to make a living. In dry years when food ran short, some nomads raided the small coastal settlements along the Mediterranean as well as the desert oases that were gradually becoming centers of trade and agriculture.

For centuries, the Imazighan also attacked Egypt, an empire based in the valley of the Nile River of northeastern Africa. In 950 B.C., an Imazighan leader seized the Egyptian throne and ruled as the pharoah (king) Shishonk I. The Egyptians knew these peoples as the Lebu, or Libyans, and gave the name Libya to the region where they lived—northern Africa west of the Nile River.

Phoenician and Greek Settlement

Around 1300 B.C., Phoenicians from what is now the Middle Eastern nation of Lebanon began building settlements along the coast of northern Africa. After making treaties with the Imazighan, the Phoenicians began trading with them. Imazighan caravans brought ivory, gold, and slaves from the African interior and sold them to the Phoenicians in exchange for imports from other Mediterranean ports. The towns of Oea, Labdah, and Sabratah—known to the Phoenicians as Tripolis (three cities)—grew along natural harbors of the coast. The area surrounding these cities became known as Tripolitania. By the fifth century B.C., busy trade had made the Phoenicians in Tripolitania wealthy and powerful.

At the same time, the Greeks of southeastern Europe were founding colonies in a region known as Cyrenaica (now eastern Libya), which took its name from the Greek settlement of Cyrene. In 631 B.C., immigrants from the Greek island of Thera built Euhesperides (modern Benghazi) and the port of Apollonia (modern

Susah). These cities thrived as trade and agriculture flourished in the region. The bustling city of Cyrene became the site of a medical school and a well-known Greek academy.

Far to the southwest, in an area called Fezzan, a Berber people known as the Garamantes were building their capital at the oasis of Germa. Archaeologists have found elaborate tombs and ruins in

Apollonia *(left)*, a port city in Cyrenaica built by the Greeks in the seventh century B.C., included a theater, a gymnasium, courtyards, public baths, and places of worship. At the same time, Phoenicians *(below)*—who also had settled in northern Libya—carried on a thriving trade with peoples in various Mediterranean ports.

21

Germa, where the Garamantes controlled the busy caravan trade between central Africa and Phoenician-held Tripolitania.

Romans Arrive

Carthage (a Phoenician city near what is now Tunis, Tunisia) faced a strong rival in Rome, a republic based across the Mediterranean on the Italian Peninsula. In the third century B.C., Carthage and Rome fought the Punic Wars in North Africa and southern Europe. This series of clashes ended with a Roman victory in 146 B.C. To ensure that Roman power would go un-challenged in the Mediterranean, the Roman leaders ordered the complete destruction of Carthage.

Although they had defeated the Carthaginians, the Romans found that they could not subdue the Imazighan, whom they and the Greeks referred to as Berbers. To keep Roman influence strong in the region, the Roman leaders formed an alliance with the Berber king of Numidia (a realm in the Upper Nile Valley) and allowed him to rule Tripolitania.

The Roman emperor Julius Caesar, seeing northern Africa as a valuable region and fearing the Numidian kings as

Photo © Betty Crowell

The ruins of Sabratah lie near modern Tripoli. Although founded by Phoenicians, Sabratah became an important Roman city beginning in the first century B.C.

Leptis Magna, a Roman city built on the ruins of Labdah (one of three ancient Phoenician settlements that together were known as Tripolis, or three cities), flourished during the first and second centuries A.D. The most well-known and impressive building left by the Romans is the theater *(above)*, where plays and musical performances took place.

dangerous rivals, deposed the ruler of Tripolitania in 46 B.C. Rome annexed (took over) Cyrenaica as well as Tripolitania and established the new Roman province of Africa Nova.

The Third Legion, an army of 12,000 Roman soldiers, arrived to stifle Berber revolts and to settle the province. To protect Africa Nova from potential enemies in the south, the Third Legion began constructing a chain of forts that stretched southward into the Sahara Desert.

Roman engineers built vast irrigation networks to supply fresh water to new towns, ports, and farms. Roman settlers cleared vast acreages in the plains and mountains of Tripolitania. Using local residents as forced laborers, the new Roman estates supplied the empire with huge crops of fruit, vegetables, grain, wine, and olive oil. The Romans also oversaw the building of new transportation routes, including the first passageway developed across the Sirte. A network of roads eventually linked Roman towns both along the Mediterranean coast and inland. In these urban areas, the Latin language and other aspects of Roman culture—including art, architecture, and religion—took hold.

Caravans that once had supplied Carthaginian ports now brought valuable trade goods such as precious stones, ivory, and slaves. They also sold wild animals to entertain the Romans in their public circuses and amphitheaters. Goods transported southward through the Sahara included wine, cloth, pottery, and glass. Trade increased with the introduction of the camel, a hardy beast of burden that originated in Asia. Able to travel long distances with little water or food, camels became the fastest and most reliable means of transporting goods across the desert.

DIVISION AND FALL OF THE ROMAN EMPIRE

Cyrenaica remained prosperous under Roman rule, although fighting between the Romans and the region's other residents regularly occurred. In the first century A.D., thousands of Jewish refugees arrived from Palestine (a land northeast of Egypt), where they had unsuccessfully revolted against Roman rule. Many of these Jews lived as nomads alongside the Berbers in desert areas, eventually converting large numbers of Berbers to Judaism, the Jewish religion.

In A.D. 115, a new revolt against Roman rule among the Jews in Cyrenaica brought a violent reaction from Rome. In retaliation a Roman army killed thousands of Jews and forced many more to flee. Although Rome prevailed, the revolt destroyed Cyrene and Cyrenaica's other large cities.

By the fourth century A.D., the people of Africa Nova were adopting another religion—Christianity. This new faith from

When Jews in Cyrenaica revolted against Roman rule in A.D. 115, the fighting killed thousands of people and destroyed the city of Cyrene (right). Although officials attempted to rebuild the city, by the fourth century no one lived there.

Murzuq was an important stop on caravan trade routes for many centuries. Like other Saharan oases, Murzuq was ruled and populated by Berbers.

the Middle East spread rapidly among the Roman residents and Greek-speaking inhabitants of North Africa. A Roman bishop, or church leader, became the spiritual head of the province of Africa Nova. Although most Romans accepted the new faith, most Berbers resisted it.

Conflict within the Roman Empire brought a division of the realm in 395. The Western Roman Empire, with its capital in Rome, took control of Tripolitania and the coast to the west. Cyrenaica, on the other hand, was ruled by the Eastern Roman (Byzantine) Empire, which had its capital at Constantinople (modern Istanbul, Turkey).

The Romans had never conquered the Garamantes, nor most Berber tribes of the Sahara. These peoples still traveled freely in the oases of the south. Berber tribes

formed confederations that governed the Saharan peoples. In the fifth century, with the Roman Empire divided and weakened, the Berbers allied with the Vandals, a Germanic tribe from northern Europe.

The Vandals arrived in Africa in 429 and began to conquer Roman towns and farms. By the mid-fifth century, the Vandals were firmly in control of Tripolitania. As the Vandals took over the property of wealthy Romans, Berbers and other non-Romans—who had been forced to work as agricultural laborers under Roman rule—left the farms to find jobs. Free from Roman rule, Tripolitanians abandoned the Christian religion, the Latin tongue, and other Roman ways of life.

After making northern Africa their base, the Vandals headed across the Mediterranean to overrun the Roman cities of

25

Italy and southern Europe. Unable to withstand these attacks, the Western Roman Empire collapsed in 476. Despite the fall of the Western Roman Empire, the Byzantine Empire remained in control of Cyrenaica and much of the eastern Mediterranean.

The Byzantine general Belisarius reached the Libyan coast in 533 and soon conquered the Vandals. Byzantine emperors restored the Latin tongue and the Christian faith in North Africa, but Byzantine rule did not extend beyond the cities of the coast. Careless Byzantine leaders mismanaged North Africa, causing unrest among both Berbers and colonists. The Byzantines collected high taxes, created laws governing religious practices, and treated their armies poorly.

Berber forces pressed their attacks as the Byzantine armies struggled to keep order. By the mid-seventh century, Berber and other African groups had established their own kingdoms and were asserting control over parts of Cyrenaica and Tripolitania. The lack of unity among the peoples of what is now Libya left the region open to new invasions and new influences.

The Coming of Islam

One of these new influences was Islam, a new faith introduced by Muhammad, an Arab who lived in what is now Saudi Arabia in the seventh century. According to Islam, the will of God governed the morals of the individual as well as the laws of the state. God's will was set forth in the Koran, the Islamic holy book. Among Muhammad's followers, called Muslims, the Koran became the basis for a new code of civil law known as sharia.

Muhammad commanded Muslims to spread their beliefs both through military conquest and peaceful conversion. By 642, 10 years after Muhammad's death, the Arab leader Omar ibn al-As and his forces had overrun Cyrenaica. Two years later, the Arabs also drove the Byzantine armies from their strongholds in Tripolitania. In the 660s, the region of Fezzan came under Arab attack. Yet the inhabitants of Fezzan resisted Arab domination and defended their historical independence.

The Arabs eventually converted many Berbers of northern Libya to Islam. The Arab conquest also brought new legal and governmental systems to North Africa. Sharia became the law of the land. Emirs (rulers) governed the provinces as representatives of the caliph of Damascus, a city in present-day Syria. The caliph was the supreme ruler over any territory that had come under Arab rule.

The Byzantine general Belisarius (shown here carrying a child) defeated the Vandals in Libya in 534. Byzantine rule only lasted about 100 years until Arab newcomers took control of the region.

Muhammad, the founder of the Islamic faith, was said to have been visited by an angel who called him the prophet of God.

In cities along the North African coast, Arabs emerged as a powerful class of merchants, traders, and officials. Arabic became the most common language in urban areas. Arab merchants gradually took control of trans-Saharan commerce and spread Islam along the caravan routes that reached southward through Fezzan. Saharan Berbers accepted the Islamic faith and adapted it to fit with their traditions, but they continued to fight against Arab control.

New Dynasties

Largely free of Arab rule, the nomadic peoples of the Sahara formed new confederations, including the Zenata and the Lawata, for mutual defense. The chaos brought by the fall of Rome and by successive conquests of Vandals, Byzantines, and Arabs enabled these confederations to maintain complete control over the oasis towns of the Sahara.

Some Berber groups joined in an anti-Arab movement centered in the oasis of Zawila. Abu al-Khattab, a leader of an Islamic sect opposed to the Damascus caliph, made Zawila his capital in about 760. The Bani Khattab, followers of Abu al-Khattab, made this oasis in Fezzan an important center of the Saharan slave trade. His missionaries also carried Islam southward through the desert into the central African plains and forests.

The Saharan traders made it possible for oases such as Zawila to flourish. The people of the oases exchanged their salt, dates, and grain for tools, weapons, livestock, and leather goods. From central Africa, ivory, ostrich feathers, civet (a substance used in perfumes), gold, precious stones, and slaves arrived by caravan before moving on to the towns of the north.

SUNNIS AND SHIITES

Despite Arab success in spreading Islam, many conflicts divided Muslims. Islam had split into Sunni and Shiite branches. Sunni Muslims were those who supported the election of Arab nobles to the caliphate (seat of Islamic leadership). Shiite Muslims believed in rule only by the descendants of Muhammad. These divisions within the religion led to further conflict in North Africa.

27

In 800 the Sunni Aghlabid dynasty (family of rulers) arose in Kairouan in what is now Tunisia. With the support of a powerful military force, the Aghlabids ruled Tunisia as well as part of Tripolitania. Under stable Aghlabid rule, the people of Tripolitania rebuilt farms, repaired roads, and restored irrigation works.

But in the early tenth century, a revolt by Shiite Muslims ended Aghlabid authority in Tripolitania. The head of this revolt, Ubaidalla Said, was known as the Mahdi to his followers, many of whom were Berbers. Said founded a new dynasty, the Fatimids—named for Fatima, the daughter of Muhammad, from whom Said claimed descent.

In 969 the forces of the Mahdi drove into Egypt, where they set up their capital in Cairo on the banks of the Nile River. The Fatimids relied on a Berber clan called the Zirids to control the vast region west of Egypt. In 1049 Zirid leaders in Tripolitania and Cyrenaica proclaimed a return to the Sunni branch and revolted against Fatimid rule.

Bedouin Invasions

To punish the Zirids and to regain their hold over North Africa, the Fatimid rulers invited the Bani Hilal and the Bani Sulaim, two powerful Arab clans from the Arabian Peninsula, to invade northern Africa in the eleventh century. Also known as the Bedouin, these nomadic Arabian peoples swept westward across North Africa, destroying farms and cities in Cyrenaica and in Tripolitania.

Many inhabitants of the coastal cities were killed or driven away from their homes into the Sahara Desert. Settled farmers were forced to become nomads again, when the Bedouin seized grazing land for their own herds. The Bedouin absorbed many of the Berbers and made the Arabic language the universal tongue of the peoples inhabiting Libya. The Bani Sulaim settled permanently in these lands,

Photo © Betty Crowell

Arabs invaded Tripolitania (the northwestern region of Libya) and took much of the prime agricultural land on the Gefara Plain. Berbers, who had been living in the area, moved up to the hills of the Jabal Nafusah. Berber villages in the region had granaries, where grain was stored in stacked compartments made of mud and stone.

and the clan divisions and family groups they established remained the most important social divisions in Libya into the twentieth century. The Bani Hilal continued westward across the Maghrib (an Arabic word meaning west)—an area encompassing Morocco, Algeria, Tunisia, and Tripolitania.

In the mid-1100s, the Almohads—a Berber dynasty from the west—pushed across North Africa as far east as Tripolitania. With its base across the Mediterranean Sea in Spain, the Almohad Empire was forced to stretch its resources over a vast area. Eventually, the Almohads lost their hold over Morocco and Spain. In the

This nobleman was a member of the Hafsid dynasty (family of rulers). Based in Tunisia, the Hafsids also governed parts of Algeria and Tripolitania.

east, the Almohad leader Muhammad ibn Abu Hafs was able to maintain control and set up a new Hafsid dynasty. Under Hafsid rule, trade and culture flourished in Tripoli and in other coastal cities of the Maghrib.

Meanwhile in Fezzan, Sharif al-Din Karakush—a member of a military caste known as the Mamluks—defeated the Bani Khattab in 1172. This event allowed the rulers of Bornu (a Saharan realm in what is now Niger) to extend their control into Fezzan and as far north as the Sirte. In Cyrenaica Bedouin clans refused to acknowledge any outside rule. They lived mainly by charging protection fees from trade caravans traveling from Egypt to the Maghrib. But after the Mamluks overthrew the sultan (ruler) of Egypt in 1250, Mamluk dynasties claimed Cyrenaica. Nevertheless, the Mamluks had little control in the sparsely populated region, where the Bedouin carefully guarded their independence.

Spaniards and Turks

Although Islam had reached into southern Europe, Christianity had taken hold throughout the rest of the European continent by 1500. The rising power of Christian nations—mainly Spain—began to threaten Tripolitania in the early sixteenth century. In 1510 a Spanish army attacked and looted Tripoli. Ferdinand, the king of Spain, later turned the city over to the Knights of St. John, a Christian military brotherhood that was contesting Islamic control of the Mediterranean.

To counter European attacks, leaders from Muslim strongholds in the Maghrib strengthened fortifications in the major port cities along the African coast of the Mediterranean. For several centuries, this region—called the Barbary Coast—played host to continuous raids, attacks, and lootings by rival corsairs, or pirates, from North Africa. From Algiers, Algeria, for example, Khayr al-Din—also known as Barbarossa (Red Beard)—launched raids on European ships in the Mediterranean. Barbarossa extended his control over much of the Maghrib and declared the territory part of the Ottoman Empire, a Muslim realm based in modern Turkey.

In 1551 an Ottoman Turkish fleet of corsairs captured Tripoli from the Knights of St. John. The next year, the Turkish sultan appointed Darghut as the pasha (governor) of Tripolitania. The busy harbor of

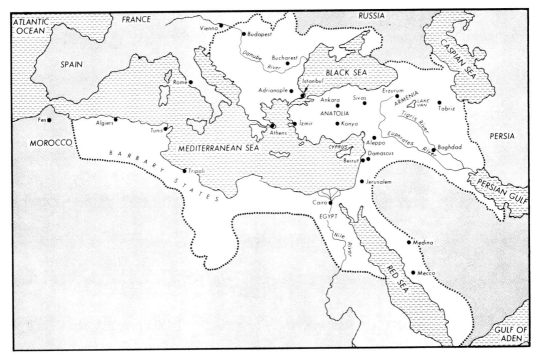

By the middle of the seventeenth century, the Ottoman Empire included much of the North African coast, all of the Middle East, and most of eastern Europe. (Map taken from *The Area Handbook for the Republic of Turkey*, 1973.)

Tripoli and the surrounding area became an Ottoman regency, or province.

The Turks defended their new conquests with an elite non-Arab corps of military officers known as Janissaries. Under the rule of deys (junior officers), the Janissaries formed a powerful class that was independent of the pasha. The result was increasing conflict between civil and military authority in Tripolitania. In 1611 the deys of Tripolitania overthrew the pasha. For the next century, the leaders of the Janissaries held power in Tripoli, the only city of substantial size in the province.

THE CORSAIRS

Under Ottoman rule, Tripoli remained an important market for goods brought by caravan from the Sahara and central Africa. But the city's principal business became the trade in stolen goods and hostages taken by corsairs in the Mediterranean Sea. These corsairs, who sailed from ports all along the Barbary Coast,

turned over part of their profits to the sultan, the pashas, and the deys. Although European nations often bombarded Tripoli in retaliation for piracy, they also paid regular tributes to Tripoli's rulers for the safe passage of European ships through Mediterranean waters.

By the late seventeenth century, political struggles among the deys of Tripoli were weakening the hold of the Ottoman Empire over the Barbary Coast. A series of deys held power, each lasting only a short time in office before being assassinated or driven out by a rival. As the situation became more chaotic, Turkish power in Tripoli gradually declined.

In 1711 a Turkish cavalry leader named Ahmad Karamanli attacked Tripoli and overthrew the dey. The sultan agreed to recognize Karamanli as an independent ruler, a move that allowed Karamanli to establish a hereditary monarchy. Unlike the deys, Karamanli established good relations with the mainly Arab population of

Tripoli. He took control of the corsairs of Tripoli and forged alliances with the nomadic confederations of the interior. He also extended his rule to Cyrenaica by appointing members of his family to govern that region.

The Karamanli dynasty encouraged trade and supported a private fleet of corsairs that operated out of Tripoli. But as trans-Mediterranean trade increased, European and North American merchants became less willing to pay for passage. Navies from Europe and the United States began fighting piracy by bombing the port of Tripoli. The U.S. government had previously paid Karamanli large sums of money in return for the promise that Tripoli's corsairs would not attack U.S. ships. In 1801, to end this yearly tribute,

the United States mounted a blockade of Tripoli to prevent goods from flowing in and out of the port. Four years later, a force of U.S. marines attacked by land across Cyrenaica and captured the town of Darnah.

Because of U.S. pressure, piracy in the Mediterranean gradually ceased, and European countries stopped paying tributes. This change greatly weakened Tripoli's economy, while higher taxes levied by the Karamanlis sparked growing civil unrest against the dynasty.

In 1832 Yusuf Karamanli gave up the throne to his son, Ali. As the dynasty's control over Tripolitania waned, Ali feared European conquest. He asked the Ottoman sultan Muhammad II for assistance to protect Tripoli. The sultan sent

European and U.S. merchants had to pay large sums of money to leaders on the Barbary Coast for protection against piracy. U.S. forces bombed the port of Tripoli in the early 1800s to end piracy and tribute payments in the Mediterranean Sea.

European Powers in Africa

(Late 1800s and Early 1900s)

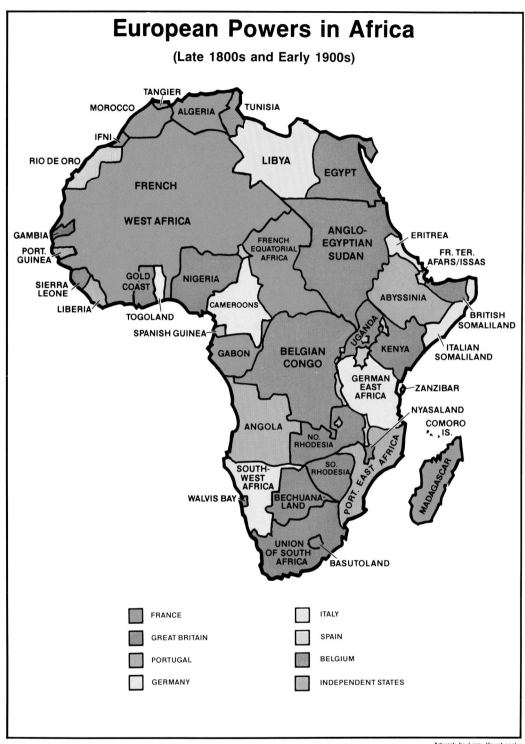

TANGIER

MOROCCO · ALGERIA · TUNISIA

IFNI

RIO DE ORO

LIBYA · EGYPT

FRENCH

WEST AFRICA

GAMBIA

PORT. GUINEA

SIERRA LEONE

LIBERIA

GOLD COAST · NIGERIA

TOGOLAND

SPANISH GUINEA

FRENCH EQUATORIAL AFRICA

ANGLO-EGYPTIAN SUDAN

ERITREA

FR. TER. AFARS/ISSAS

ABYSSINIA

BRITISH SOMALILAND

CAMEROONS

GABON · BELGIAN CONGO

UGANDA · KENYA

ITALIAN SOMALILAND

GERMAN EAST AFRICA

ZANZIBAR

NYASALAND

COMORO IS.

ANGOLA

NO. RHODESIA

SOUTH-WEST AFRICA

SO. RHODESIA

PORT. EAST AFRICA

MADAGASCAR

WALVIS BAY

BECHUANA-LAND

UNION OF SOUTH AFRICA

BASUTOLAND

FRANCE

GREAT BRITAIN

PORTUGAL

GERMANY

ITALY

SPAIN

BELGIUM

INDEPENDENT STATES

Artwork by Larry Kaushansky

By the late nineteenth century, European nations had carved the continent of Africa into areas of influence. Italy began its conquest of Libya in 1911 and held control of the country until 1947. (Map information taken from *The Anchor Atlas of World History*, 1978.)

troops to reinstate Ottoman control in Tripolitania. To ensure that the region would remain part of the Ottoman Empire, Muhammad II forced Ali into exile and in 1835 made Tripolitania an Ottoman province under a Turkish governor.

The Sanusi Brotherhood

Libya's Turkish governors were wary of the growing influence of European powers such as France, which conquered and colonized Algeria in the 1830s. The Turks also feared the newly independent government in Cairo that had overthrown Turkish authority in Egypt. Within Libya the governors also faced frequent revolts and warfare among the clans that sought control of the Saharan trade routes.

During this time of weakening Turkish power, the Islamic scholar and holy man Sidi Muhammad Ali al-Sanusi came to Libya from his home in Algeria. A renowned student of the Koran, Sidi Muhammad (known as the Grand Sanusi) favored a return to traditional Islam as it had been practiced by Muhammad and his followers in the seventh century. In 1837 he organized the Sanusi brotherhood in the holy city of Mecca, in what is now Saudi Arabia.

The Grand Sanusi eventually settled in the highlands of the Jabal al-Akhdar in Cyrenaica, where he founded a series of *zawiya,* or holy lodges. These lodges, headed by a spiritual leader known as a sheikh, functioned as monasteries, schools, courts, and places of pilgrimage for the members of the Sanusi brotherhood. Gradually, the Sanusis brought unity to the many feuding clans of the desert. They also organized an effective resistance to the Turks and to European colonial powers.

The Grand Sanusi's son Sidi Muhammad al-Mahdi became the leader of the Sanusi movement upon his father's death in 1859. Al-Mahdi led the brotherhood to the height of its power and prestige in the eastern Sahara. He moved the Sanusi headquarters to the Kufra Oasis in southeastern Cyrenaica, where a newly established zawiya became an important hub of guerrilla forces fighting against British colonists in Sudan and Egypt. Meanwhile, French advances from the west and from the south threatened Tripolitania and Fezzan.

Italian Colonization

But Britain and France were not the only European powers interested in northern Africa. In the late nineteenth century, archaeologists uncovered extensive Roman ruins underneath the sands of northern Libya. This event prompted many Italian leaders to claim that Libya, as an ancient Roman province, rightfully belonged under Italian rule. Italian banks and export companies built branch offices in Tripoli, and the Italian government invested money to improve roads and ports in the area. In 1911 Italian forces captured Tripoli and several ports in Cyrenaica.

To fight the growing influence of Italy, the Turks organized and armed Arab nomads and villagers in the countryside. But Turkish power in the Mediterranean was continuing to weaken, and Turkey soon recognized the independence of Cyrenaica and Tripolitania. Italy then brought these regions under Italian rule.

Meanwhile, the Sanusi zawiya became the centers of armed resistance to the Italian colonial government. Sanusi forces defeated the Italian army in Fezzan in 1914, and Sanusi guerrillas also campaigned successfully against the Italians in the Sirte. Despite Sanusi successes inland, Italy remained in firm control of the growing cities and farmland of the coast. The Italian government began moving Italian farmers into Tripolitania to relieve unemployment and social unrest within Italy, an action that prompted growing unrest among Tripolitanians forced to move from their land.

At the same time Italy was involved in Libya, the Italian troops were forced to shift their attention. In 1914 World War I erupted in Europe. Germany allied with the Ottoman Empire and fought against the Allies—Italy, Britain, France, and the United States. To carry on their campaign against Italian occupation, the Sanusis allied with the Germans. Sanusi fighters attacked British forces in Egypt, which had become a British protectorate, but in 1916 Britain drove the Sanusi brotherhood out of Egypt and continued on in search of the Sanusi leader. This leader, Ahmad al-Sharif, fled Libya and passed along his title to his cousin, Sidi Muhammad Idris. Britain agreed to a truce with Idris and recognized him as the emir of Cyrenaica.

When World War I ended in 1918 with an Allied victory, Italy again claimed Tripolitania and Cyrenaica as its colonies and put Fezzan under military rule. The Italians confirmed Idris as the leader of Cyrenaica, where the Sanusi brotherhood was strongest. This area remained largely independent of Italian control. In 1922 leaders of a Libyan nationalist movement in Tripolitania proposed that Idris become emir of Tripolitania as well as Cyrenaica. Although he accepted, Idris soon fled to Egypt to avoid being captured by the Italians.

Guerrilla War

After its defeat in World War I, the Ottoman Empire collapsed and was replaced by the Turkish Republic. In 1923 Turkey signed a postwar treaty surrendering its former Ottoman territories, which the Allies scrambled to divide among themselves. Italy, for example, formally laid claim to Libya. But in Libya, guerrilla warfare against Italian rule continued. A Bedouin Sanusi scholar named Omar Mukhtar became a national resistance leader. Mukhtar organized hit-and-run attacks carried out by his Bedouin followers,

who escaped into the desert after raiding ports and settlements along the coast.

The Italians carried on a bloody campaign to defeat the Sanusi guerrillas and to destroy their support among the Bedouin nomads. The regime set up a barbed-wire barrier along the Egyptian border to prevent guerrillas from crossing into Egypt for supplies. By blocking wells, killing livestock, and destroying pasture, the Italians forced many Bedouin into exile. Others who stayed in Libya ended up in refugee camps, where thousands died of illness and starvation. Their traditional grazing lands were turned over to Italian farmers, who benefited from new irrigation projects carried out by the colonial government.

During the 1920s and 1930s, Italy built new roads and railroads, irrigation works, apartment and office buildings, and port facilities in Libya. A modern route—the Litoranea—was laid across the Sirte to facilitate transportation between Tripolitania and Cyrenaica. By ordering these projects, Benito Mussolini, the dictator of Italy, sought to encourage poor, jobless, and landless Italians to move to Libya. Thousands of new settlers arrived, while many Libyans lost their lands and lived in poverty.

In 1931 the Italian colonial government captured Omar Mukhtar and executed him in a public square in Benghazi. Mukhtar's death ended most Sanusi resistance. By 1934 Italy had firm control of both Tripolitania and Cyrenaica and formally joined the colonies as Libya. Fezzan remained a separate military province, where a general council replaced traditional tribal councils. In 1939 Italy annexed Libya, placing it under direct rule for the first time.

World War II and Independence

Once again, while Italy concentrated on events in Libya, rumblings of war were beginning in Europe. In September 1939,

In the 1930s, the Italian government transported more than 110,000 poor Italians *(above)* to Libya, where they were given free farmland taken from Bedouin herders. Besides offering land, the colonial officials authorized the building of new Italian-style housing developments and issued mules, carts, and furniture to the settlers *(below)*.

Germany attacked the central European nation of Poland, sparking World War II. Britain and France again found themselves fighting against Germany. (The Soviet Union and the United States would later join the Allied effort.) Italy, which sided with Germany in an alliance known as the Axis, entered the war against Britain the next year.

Although begun in Europe, the conflict eventually spread to European colonial holdings in North Africa. As a result, Libyan nationalists saw an opportunity for overthrowing Italian rule and met in Egypt to discuss Libya's future. At the meeting, Idris again was declared the leader of both Tripolitania and Cyrenaica. He allied his forces with those of Britain, which still held Egypt as a colony. Libyan volunteers joined British units fighting in North Africa.

In September 1940, Italy invaded Egypt from its bases in Libya. German reinforcements arrived in 1941, but the stronger British forces pushed the Axis troops back into Cyrenaica. For months German and British troops struggled in the deserts of Cyrenaica, where the battle lines shifted back and forth until early 1942. By October, Britain had defeated the Axis forces in North Africa, Germany and Italy had pulled out, and British forces were occupying Libya.

The fighting had destroyed towns, had devastated farms, and had driven thousands of refugees from Cyrenaica. As farmers abandoned their fields, the people of the region once again turned to raising livestock. Poor and sparsely populated, Libya remained under British military administration until the end of the war in 1945.

In 1947 Italy signed a treaty giving up all of its claims to Libya. To decide Libya's future, the United Nations (UN) formed a series of committees. A special commission, for example, drew up a new constitution for an independent Libyan government. The new constitution established a hereditary monarchy, a two-house legislature, a prime minister, and a council of ministers.

Photo by UPI/Bettmann Newsphotos

In Libya during World War II, Allied troops (which included soldiers from Britain, France, and the United States) inspected a bombed-out German anti-aircraft weapon in the Sahara. The Allies won the war in 1945.

Sidi Muhammad Idris, the former emir of Cyrenaica, was named king of Libya in 1950. One year later, Idris proclaimed Libya's independence.

The members of the UN agreed to allow Libya's independence, which officially took effect on December 24, 1951.

After returning from exile, Sidi Muhammad Idris became king of Libya. As one of his first official acts, the new king outlawed political parties. To promote the Libyan economy, Idris maintained friendly relations with UN member nations, especially the United States and Britain, both of which contributed money to Libya for industrial development. In return, Idris allowed the two nations to build military bases along the Mediterranean coast. The king's agreements with Britain and the United States angered many Libyans, who believed these arrangements kept their country under the influence of foreign powers.

Economic and Political Shifts

In 1959 engineers discovered large reserves of underground crude oil in Cyrenaica, and several foreign drilling companies rushed in to build wells. The Libyan government signed agreements with these firms in exchange for 50 percent of the oil profits. The government planned new social services and construction projects as oil income began to enrich the nation's treasury.

Although more money was flowing into Libya, much of the vast sum earned from oil financed Idris's large and inefficient government. Many of the new developments went unfinished. Idris began to lose popularity as his government failed to implement development plans in Libya. In addition, Idris did little to ally with other

Muslim nations, with which many Libyans felt linked politically and spiritually.

The 1967 military success of Israel, a Jewish state in the Middle East, against Egypt and other Arab states encouraged members of the Libyan army and of the middle class to reject Idris, who kept Libya out of the war. They saw the Libyan monarchy as corrupt, overly friendly to the United States and Britain, and not allied strongly enough with the Arab states of the Middle East.

Within the small Libyan army, a revolutionary underground group called the Free Officers' movement gained new followers. Dedicated to overthrowing the Libyan monarchy, the movement was led by Muammar el-Qaddafi, a member of the nomadic Qaddafa tribe of the Sirte Desert.

In his youth, Qaddafi had been inspired by the nationalist Arab hero Gamal Abdel Nasser, who led a strongly anticolonial government in Egypt. Driven by the goal of a single, united Arab nation that would stretch across North Africa, Qaddafi planned for the dethroning of Idris and the expulsion of all U.S. and British interests from the Arab world.

With his allies in the armed forces, Qaddafi formed the Revolutionary Command Council (RCC) to prepare for a takeover of the Libyan government. On September 1, 1969, while Idris was out of the country, Qaddafi and his supporters seized government and military buildings in Tripoli and Benghazi. Libyan civilians and members of the military put up little resistance to the coup d'etat (forceful takeover).

Libya under Qaddafi

The 12-member RCC established the Socialist Libyan Arab Republic and appointed Qaddafi as prime minister and head of the armed forces. The RCC abolished the monarchy and the national legislature and named itself as the new governing organization.

Under Qaddafi the RCC turned Libya into a socialist state based on Islamic law. The new government created state-owned enterprises that were managed by committees of workers. Qaddafi also nationalized, or put under state control, mosques and Islamic lodges and banned the Sanusi order to enforce greater loyalty to his regime. In addition, foreign oil operations in Libya were placed under Libyan control. Jews and Italians were expelled from the country, and their property was confiscated. The United States and Britain closed their military bases, prompting the Libyan government to declare a national holiday.

The RCC also set up new administrative boundaries. The new provinces crossed ancient borders recognized by Libya's vari-

Photo by Archive Photos

Muammar el-Qaddafi led the Revolutionary Command Council—a group of young army officers and soldiers—in the overthrow of the Libyan government in 1969.

In the early 1970s, Qaddafi's regime began a cultural revolution designed to modify Libyan society. Although many of the new laws were restrictive, Libyan women benefited from some of the changes. Besides gaining the freedom to wear whatever they wanted, women were encouraged to pursue educational opportunities, to take jobs, and to participate in politics.

Photo by Dick Bancroft

ous clans and tribes. As a result, the chiefs of these groups lost much of their power to newly formed committees and local governments. These people's committees took control of businesses, local governments, universities, and factories in large cities as well as in small villages. All political parties were outlawed, except for the Arab Socialist Union, which supported the goals of the revolutionary government.

Libya's government spearheaded a cultural revolution in the early 1970s, with the goal of further transforming Libya into a purely Arab, socialist state. Sharia was strictly enforced. Arabic—spoken by nearly all Libyans—was declared the nation's official language, and the government banned nightclubs, the use of alcohol, and certain books. The RCC took control of radio and television stations, newspapers, and other forms of communication. Opponents of the Qaddafi regime were jailed, sentenced to death, or forced into exile.

Some of the changes made by Qaddafi distanced Libyan society from Islamic traditions. Women in Libya, for instance, began to enjoy equal status with men in the 1970s—a change that was uncommon among Arab nations. The RCC expanded women's rights in marriage and divorce. Women were encouraged to attend school and were permitted to get jobs. Qaddafi also made economic reforms. The regime nationalized many businesses. New laws set limits on the amount of property individuals could own. Oil revenues were used to build and maintain new roads, schools, health facilities, and public housing.

Qaddafi also began working with other Arab nations to create a pan-Arab federation. In 1971 Egypt, Libya, and Syria agreed to unify their governments. But Anwar el-Sadat, the Egyptian leader, and Qaddafi did not see eye to eye on a timetable for the merger, and the unification never took place. In fact, relations between Sadat and Qaddafi grew hostile, and fighting between the two countries broke out in 1977.

By the late 1970s, the United States and most European nations had ended diplomatic relations with Libya. Egypt, Tunisia, Chad, and Syria also distanced themselves from the Libyan government. The leaders of these Arab nations believed Qaddafi encouraged terrorist groups that sought to overthrow their governments. For example, after sending troops to occupy the

39

Aozou Strip, a mineral-rich territory lying along Libya's border with Chad, Qaddafi sent antigovernment rebels in northern Chad money, equipment, and troops. Libya was also accused of contributing money, weapons, training, and explosives to support terrorist activities around the world.

Recent Events

Tensions with Europe and the United States worsened in the 1980s. After a series of terrorist incidents in Europe were linked to Qaddafi, the U.S. government sent naval forces into the Gulf of Sirte to defy Libya's claim to these waters. In April 1986, U.S. forces destroyed several Libyan gunboats and planes in the area, and U.S. bombers attacked Qaddafi's

headquarters near Tripoli. Critics of the U.S. attack suggested that conflicting evidence about Libya's role in past terrorist attacks made it difficult to pin the blame on Qaddafi. Some international observers feared that violent retaliations against Libya would only result in more terrorism.

After the U.S. attack on Tripoli, Libyan agents were accused of bombing a Pan Am jetliner over Scotland in 1988 as well as a French airplane over Niger in 1989. Qaddafi repeatedly refused to surrender for trial the suspects in these bomb attacks, claiming the men would not receive fair trials. In response, the U.S. government encouraged the UN Security Council to approve economic sanctions against Libya. The penalties included a ban on air traffic in and out of the country and a halt

Photo by AP/World Wide Photos

Evidence linked Qaddafi to the 1986 attack on a bar in Germany *(above)* **that was popular among U.S. soldiers. As a result, U.S. officials sent military aircraft to bomb targets in Libya, including Qaddafi's home** *(right).*

Photo by Dick Bancroft

to the sale of military equipment to Libya. The Security Council toughened the sanctions in 1992, preventing Libya from accessing its money in foreign bank accounts and stopping some sales of oil-production equipment.

As a result of the economic sanctions, Libya's oil-producing facilities began to suffer from disrepair and lack of parts, and factories became unable to operate at full capacity. In addition, a drop in the international price of oil further damaged the Libyan economy. Meanwhile, some Libyans—within and outside of the country—demonstrated increasing resistance to the Qadaffi regime. From exile many opponents called for the overthrow of the government. Islamic fundamentalists, who called for a return to the moral and legal principles of early Islam, also opposed Qaddafi's regime and have taken part in antigovernment demonstrations.

Libya began to address its economic problems in the early 1990s. Some businesses were returned to private ownership, and restrictions on exports and imports were relaxed. But the nation still depends on oil for nearly all of its export income. As a result, its ability to provide extensive social services is tied to fluctuating oil prices. Some Libyans, especially those who were hurt by Qaddafi's nationalization program of the 1970s and 1980s, remain strongly opposed to the regime. Although Libya has been isolated from Europe, the United States, and much of the Middle East by its past actions, Qaddafi remains popular among a large segment of Libyan society and among many in the armed forces.

Government

Libya's official name is the Great Socialist People's Libyan Arab Jamahiriya. Jamahiriya translates into "state of the masses," "peopledom," or "republic." After the overthrow of the monarchy in 1969, the Revolutionary Command Council became the country's governing body. Under the direction of the RCC and Qaddafi, the nation adopted the popular committee as the basic unit of government. In 1977 Libya abolished the RCC and replaced it with the General Secretariat, a ruling committee with Qaddafi as secretary-general. The legislature is known as the General People's Congress (GPC). All of the congress's 1,112 representatives—elected by local councils—are members of the Arab Socialist Union, the country's only legal political party.

The GPC members elect the General People's Committee, which includes the secretaries (heads) of 17 major ministries, including those overseeing economic affairs, public health, housing, energy, and justice. Most of these ministries are located outside of the capital, in Benghazi, Kufra, and other cities.

More than 2,000 local people's congresses govern businesses, towns, trade unions, and other institutions, such as universities. People's congresses also lead the 25 *baladiya,* or provinces. Adults over the age of 18 elect the members of these congresses. The people's congresses in turn appoint popular committees, which pass resolutions to be voted on by the GPC.

Libya's judicial system is based on sharia, or traditional Islamic law. The court system is led by a special council of judicial authorities. A supreme court in Tripoli decides important criminal and constitutional cases. Five departments, each of which has five officials, make up the supreme court.

Lower courts include courts of appeal in Benghazi, Tripoli, and Sabha. These chambers hear appeals from courts of first instance and summary courts, the country's lowest courts, which are located in almost all communities. In addition, a group of special courts supplements Libya's judicial system. A people's court hears political cases, and a number of revolutionary courts try cases involving political opponents of Qaddafi's regime.

Photo © Bernard Regent/The Hutchison Library

Most of Libya's 5.2 million citizens live in urban areas. Libya's population is small compared to those of its North African neighbors, but it has the highest population growth rate in the region.

3) The People

With the vast Sahara Desert covering most of Libya, the nation has always had a very low population density. Overall, the country averages about eight persons per square mile. In the interior, this figure falls to less than one person per square mile. But more than 90 percent of the 5.2 million Libyans live along or near the Mediterranean coast, where all of the cities and large towns have been built.

The country's low population presents the Libyan government with a serious problem. Although Libyan industries have grown with the investment of money from oil, not enough laborers have the skills necessary to run the country's factories, power plants, and businesses. As a result, the government actively supports population growth with payments to families for each child born. By the mid-1990s, this policy had led to a population growth rate of 3.4 percent, the highest in North Africa and one of the highest on the continent as a whole. In fact, by 1995 one-half of the Libyan population was under the age of 15.

42

Ethnic Groups

The majority of Libyans are Arabs, who trace their ancestry to the intermarriage of Arab and Berber groups after the Arab invasions of the seventh century. Before the 1950s, many Libyans—especially those living outside the cities—identified more strongly with their traditional clans and family groups than with the Libyan nation. The majority of the people in the country lived as nomads at least part of the year, moving their homes and flocks to different pastures as the seasons changed.

The sudden oil wealth of the 1950s and 1960s dramatically altered Libyan society. Many clans splintered as members moved into urban areas to find jobs and took up a more settled existence. To promote pan-Arab unity, Qaddafi's revolutionary government also sought to destroy clan loyalties by breaking up the clans. The government redrew political boundaries to eliminate traditional clan boundaries, and moved livestock herders into rural villages. Although some nomads still inhabit northern Libya, their numbers have been steadily falling since the 1960s. Some nomadic tribes continue to live as herders and traders in southern Libya.

Libya has several distinct ethnic groups, however. Ethnic Berbers, most of whom live in the highland regions of northern Libya, make up a small minority. Berber place-names have survived in the Jabal Nafusah. In various towns west of Tripoli, Berber dialects are commonly heard. Many Berbers support themselves as farmers or as nomadic herders and live in tents with their extended families.

The Tuareg peoples inhabit the southern and western reaches of Libya, as well as southern Algeria, northern Mali, and northern Niger. They trace their origins to a society of nomads who historically lived by raiding settlements and caravans in the Sahara Desert. These people speak Tamashek, an ancient Berber dialect, and write in an ancient geometric script known as tifinagh. Like most Libyans, the Tuareg follow Islam, but they also have developed religious and social customs of their own. For example, only women—who dominate the Tuareg economy—may own property, and inheritances are passed among female members of the family.

Tuareg men don traditional blue veils, which historically were dyed with indigo and colored their faces blue—earning them the name "blue men." More than 10,000 Tuareg people live in the Libyan section of the Sahara. With larger populations in Algeria, Niger, and Mali, the Tuareg—age-old nomadic desert herders—total more than 300,000.

The Tebu, who live in the Kufra Oasis and in the Tibesti Mountains straddling Libya and northern Chad, have been an important central Saharan group for centuries. Like the Tuareg, the Tebu historically were nomads. The Tebu are Muslims whose religious beliefs were strongly molded by the Sanusi brotherhood. Divided into at least 20 large clans, the Tebu now number about 10,000 within Libya.

Libya's mixture of Arab, Berber, Tuareg, and Tebu peoples is reflected in traditional clothing and customs. Nevertheless, virtually all Libyans share in common the Arabic language and the Islamic religion.

Photo by Archive Photos/Hirz

Photo by Dick Bancroft

Photo by Dick Bancroft

Photo by Dick Bancroft

They live in one of the most isolated regions of the Sahara and have remained largely free of outside control.

The Libyan population also includes a number of skilled and unskilled foreign workers who help Libya meet its labor needs. Egyptians, Tunisians, Italians, Indians, and British have jobs in the country's various industrial, communications, and natural resources projects. Several thousand U.S. citizens are employed in the oil industry. Tripoli has small neighborhoods of Greeks and Maltese, who work in the fishing industry.

Religion

Islam first came to Libya's coastal cities with the Arab invasions of the seventh century. Missionaries and invaders later brought this faith to the towns and oases of the interior and to the Berber nomads of the northern highlands. For many centuries, sharia was the only political or administrative system held in common by the many different clans and classes of Libyan society. In 1973, during the cultural revolution, Libya's government made sharia the basis for the country's laws and government. The state completely banned the use of alcohol, outlawed gambling, and closed all nightclubs. The regime proclaimed that all future laws would be based on the principles of Islam as explained in the Koran.

Devout Muslims pray five times each day and observe the five pillars of Islam—praying daily, fasting during the holy month of Ramadan, almsgiving to the poor, believing in Allah (God) and in the prophet Muhammad, and making a pilgrimage to the holy city of Mecca. Each Libyan village, town, and neighborhood has a mosque, to which a crier calls Muslims for prayer.

In Libya, where Islam is the official state religion, the Islamic lunar calendar is observed. Months begin with each new moon, and the years are counted from

Photo by Dick Bancroft

Dominating Tripoli's cityscape are many minarets—towers at the mosques (Islamic houses of worship) from which criers call Muslims to prayer five times a day.

Muhammad's journey from Mecca to Medina in 632. Libyans celebrate this journey, called the Hegira, each New Year's day of the lunar calendar. Mouleed—held on the birthdate of Muhammad—is a celebration of the life and faith of Muhammad. Ramadan is a holy month of prayer and

45

fasting. Muslims who observe Ramadan may not drink, smoke, or eat between sunrise and sunset. The end of Ramadan is announced with the sighting of the new moon and a feast.

Health and Education

The Qaddafi regime introduced a new system of public health care after the revolution of 1969. The state provides free health care and medicines to its citizens, as well as an extensive network of public clinics and hospitals. The country's two largest hospitals are in Tripoli and Benghazi. New medical colleges have greatly improved the ratio of doctors, dentists, and nurses to the general population. In addition, Libya has built nurseries and orphanages. Libya's infant mortality rate, an important measure of a nation's public health, stands at 68 out of every 1,000 live births—a figure slightly higher than average in North Africa but low for Africa on the whole.

The public health system in Libya provides for health insurance, old-age pensions, and payments to workers with job-related disabilities. Once dependent on their families for care, retirees now have a state-supported social-security system. Average life expectancy in Libya is 63 years, about average for northern Africa but higher than the continent's overall figure.

With a limited public education system, Libya long suffered a serious lack of trained engineers and other professionals. Before World War II, few schools of any

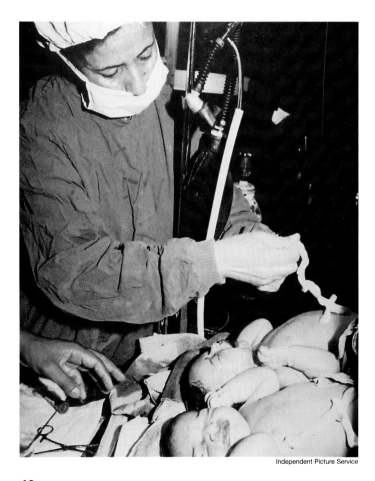

A Libyan doctor examines newborn twins. By 1995 more than half of Libya's population was under the age of 15.

Young Libyan women practice their typing skills in a business class. Since the 1970s, increasing numbers of females in Libya have been attending schools and universities.

kind existed, and those that did operate accepted only males for religious training. In the years after World War II, the literacy rate among Libyans was less than 10 percent.

Education improved greatly after the discovery of oil, which allowed new investment in schools, training centers, and universities. In the 1970s, after the revolution, more grade schools and secondary schools opened, and the percentage of Libyan children—especially female students—attending school rapidly increased. In addition, more women began enrolling in the nation's universities and training schools. In the 1990s, the country's literacy rate reached 50 percent among females and about 75 percent among males.

All children between the ages of 6 and 15 are now required to attend nine years of school or vocational training. They may then attend three years of secondary school, which includes courses in science and the humanities.

Higher education in Libya is state-controlled and is provided free of charge to students. The country's first university was established in 1955 in Benghazi. By the mid-1990s, Tripoli, Mersa Brega, and Sabha also had universities. Al-Bayda is the site of a religious institute. Vocational schools in Libya offer training in commercial, industrial, and agricultural careers. There are also state-supported religious schools and training centers for teachers.

Language, Literature, and Communications

Since 1969 the official language of Libya has been Arabic. A Semitic tongue with

47

An ornamental page from the Koran (Islamic holy book) features classical Arabic—the language used mainly by religious leaders and scholars. Most written materials use a standard literary Arabic, while everyday conversations commonly occur in local dialects.

Photo by Corbis-Bettmann

origins on the Arabian Peninsula, Arabic spread to North Africa during the Arab invasions of the seventh century. Arabic exists in many forms and has various dialects. Classical Arabic—the language of the Koran—is an international tongue used mainly by religious scholars and teachers. Journalists, schoolteachers, and scientists use literary Arabic. Within Libya, many local and regional dialects of Arabic are spoken.

Some Berbers of northwestern Libya speak both Arabic and Numidian, an ancient African language that spread north from the Upper Nile Valley of Sudan. Villagers and nomads of the Jabal Nafusah and other regions with large Berber populations also use Berber dialects. Although the state forbids street signs and advertisements in English and Italian, these and other European languages are used by some foreign workers living in Libya.

The government strictly controls the production and distribution of all printed matter, and few foreign books or magazines are available for sale. Libya's most popular book is the Koran, the Islamic holy book, which dates to the mid-seventh century. The available secular (nonreligious) literature praises the achievements of the revolutionary regime and is strongly nationalistic. Many Libyans also read *The Green Book,* a three-volume work by Muammar el-Qaddafi on the goals and ideals of his 1969 revolution.

One of the most popular communications media in Libya is the radio. There are several state-sponsored radio stations that broadcast music, news, and religious programs. A national television network broadcasts mostly foreign programs with Arabic subtitles. Magazines and daily newspapers are also available. The state's official press office, the Jamahiriya News Agency, publishes the *New Dawn* newspaper in Tripoli.

Architecture and Art

Ancient architecture in Libya includes the ruins of Sabratha, Leptis Magna, and Cyrene. The early Greek and Roman inhabitants of these cities left behind fora (public areas), theaters, baths, marketplaces, streets, shops, and homes. Archaeologists have also uncovered remains of the Garamentes civilization at the desert town of Germa. The mosques of Karamanlis and Gurgi in Tripoli are among the best examples of Islamic architecture in the country.

Libyan homes traditionally include wall and floor carpets as the main decoration. Muslims in Libya often carry a prayer rug,

Photo by Archive Photos

An old Islamic mosque gleams white under the hot sun at Zliten, a town on the Mediterranean coast between Tripoli and Misratah. Many buildings in Libya and throughout North Africa are painted white to reflect the heat.

which they use for daily prayers when they cannot get to a mosque. Although small carpet factories still operate in Misratah and other cities, state ownership of the industry has caused a decline in production.

Berber and Arabic traditions dominate Libyan art. The ancient art of the Berbers—as seen in carpets, embroidery, and jewelry—emphasizes complex shapes and lines. Forbidden by Islam from representing human or animal forms in their works, artists in Libya mainly feature intricate lines and geometric patterns and designs in carpets, metalwork, leather goods, painted wall tiles, and pottery.

Traditional folk songs and dances are popular throughout Libya. In the cities, music and dance troupes perform regularly at festivals, in ceremonies, and on television. Tuareg musicians and dancers entertain audiences in various oases of the Sahara.

Photo by Dick Bancroft

Libyans in Tripoli perform a traditional folk dance.

Libyan cooks use many spices—
such as coriander and chili powder
in the dishes they prepare.

Courtesy of Nancy Smedstad/Independent Picture Service

Food

Libyan food has much in common with the cuisines of other North African nations. Couscous, one of the most popular dishes, is also well-known in Tunisia, Algeria, and Morocco. To make couscous, cooks steam semolina (a wheat product) and serve it on a large platter with vegetables and meat. Steamed semolina also appears at breakfast mixed with honey and milk.

Libyans eat their largest meal at midday, before the day grows too hot. The most common meat is lamb, which is often cooked on a spit over an open fire. Kabob is a mixture of chunks of lamb and other meat prepared on thin skewers. *Tajine,* a meat pastry, may include mutton, lamb, beef, or chicken. *Shashokva,* roasted lamb in a tomato-based sauce, and *mouloqiyah* (steamed vegetables) are also popular. Most Libyan dishes also include a generous helping of peppers and spices.

Accompanying most Libyan meals is *kesrah,* a flat round bread. *Babaganoug—* a filling mixture of eggplant, oil, and sesame paste served with kesrah—may

Courtesy of Nancy Smedstad/Independent Picture Service

Harvested from abundant date palm trees, dates are a favorite snack in Libya. Dates are also commonly dried to be used later in recipes.

51

appear at the table at any time of the day. The evening meal is a lighter fare of fruits—grapes, oranges, or other citrus fruits—and cheese. Libyans also enjoy yogurt made from goat's milk.

Thick black coffee is served throughout the day, as is sweet mint tea. Libyans drink fruit juices and bitter, a carbonated drink. According to Islamic tradition and Libyan laws, alcoholic beverages are strictly banned.

Sports and Holidays

Young people throughout Libya play soccer in the open spaces of cities, villages, and oases. A popular team sport, soccer unites many Libyans in a shared enthusiasm, especially when the national team battles with its Middle Eastern and North African opponents. Many Libyans also like to watch the ancient sport of horse racing. Racetracks in rural areas host contests among the fastest Arabian horses, as well as among the *maharis,* or racing camels. In the cities, athletes take part in basketball, track, and boxing events.

The first Libyan Olympic athletes participated in the Mexico City Olympic Games in 1968. But a terrorist incident during the 1972 games, partially blamed on Libya's government, led to the banning of Libya from Olympic contests until 1992, when Libyan athletes again participated.

Libyans have a full calendar of national nonreligious holidays, for which they use the Gregorian calendar that most other countries use. Evacuation Day takes place on June 11. Marking the evacuation of the Wheelus Air Force Base by the United

Young Libyans play a game of wheelchair basketball. Libya has a comprehensive social service program that assists people who suffer from injury, illness, or disability.

A group of men jogs around a running track in Tripoli. Track and field events, soccer, and basketball are especially popular in urban parts of the country.

States in 1970, the holiday is considered by Libyans to be the final defeat of the colonial powers in North Africa. On September 1, the country celebrates Muammar el-Qaddafi's 1969 revolution with elaborate parades, fireworks, and speeches delivered by Qaddafi. Libya's Independence Day is December 24.

Children in Libya participate in a school performance to honor a national holiday.

Since the 1950s, when oil was discovered in Libya, Tripoli and other cities have grown into major urban centers.

4) The Economy

The discovery of oil in the late 1950s changed Libya from one of the world's poorest nations to one of the wealthiest. Oil exports brought in vast sums of money from foreign countries—mostly European nations. Libyan officials drew on this money to build an industrial economy. New factories rose in the cities, and irrigation projects expanded the amount of land available for agriculture. But many Libyans still experienced poverty and saw little improvement in their daily lives. This economic inequality was an important cause of the 1969 revolution, which the majority of Libyans supported.

The revolutionary government put into place an entirely different economic system. The new regime seized control of both foreign-owned and domestic factories, mines, oil wells, and banks. All privately held industry was outlawed. Libyans were allowed to own only the house they inhabited. The government adopted a series of five-year plans that set production goals for Libyan industries and that put each sector of the economy under central control.

Committees of workers operated both large and small companies within Libya. The government made new investments in agriculture, with the goal of making the nation self-sufficient in food. Libya also tried to develop new manufacturing firms whose exports would reduce the country's dependence on the oil market.

Although Libya greatly increased its industrial production as well as its standard of living, a fall in the price of oil during the 1980s slowed the flow of foreign money into Libya's treasury. This decline stopped many important development efforts, including projects to expand industry and to improve housing and irrigation works.

Libya also found that public ownership of businesses was leading to inefficiency and shortages in important products, including food and consumer goods. In response to these problems, the state has allowed small private shops to open and has allowed foreign oil companies to re-

turn. Libya's industries and agriculture are growing along with its population, and the country still has large reserves of oil and natural gas to draw on for export income. Yet the dependence on the changeable price of a single natural resource still causes great uncertainty in the country's economic future.

Oil and Other Mining

After the first oil fields in Tripolitania and Cyrenaica began producing, foreign companies arrived to explore Libya's deserts for other reserves. Oil production and refining quickly became the largest sector of the Libyan economy, as new fields were developed in Tripolitania and in the Gulf of Sirte. Pipelines carried crude oil to refineries at five bustling oil terminals on

Workers in Libya repair underground oil pipelines. The country's economy is dependent mainly on oil revenues to pay for food and other goods.

the Mediterranean coast. Tankers carried the refined petroleum to Europe's quickly expanding energy market.

The Libyan government grants each oil company the right to draw oil from a certain field. In return the company delivers a percentage of crude oil to Libya's state-owned oil company, which refines and markets the fuel on its own.

Libya's high-grade oil is low in sulfur, making the crude oil easy to refine and less polluting. The country's location near Europe is also an advantage, allowing Libya to transport oil more cheaply than can other oil-producing nations in the Middle East and Africa.

Natural gas, a by-product of oil drilling, is also becoming an important energy export. In 1971 Libya began storing the gas for sale instead of burning it off at the wells where it was produced. Although engineers estimate that Libya has about 25 years of oil production left in its existing deposits, the country has huge natural-gas reserves that could last for several centuries.

Libya has few mineral resources besides oil, but the state has invested in several new mining ventures. Iron ore from a large strip mine near Sabha supplies raw material to an iron and steel plant at Misratah. Workers draw salt from marshes and depressions near the coast, and small deposits of limestone, gypsum, and marble provide building materials.

Manufacturing and Trade

The 1969 revolution led to nationalization of the manufacturing firms that had been operating in Tripoli and in a few other Libyan cities. At that time, most Libyan factories processed food products, such as olive oil, beverages, and citrus fruits.

An oil tanker waits in the port at Tripoli. Libya exports almost all its oil across the Mediterranean Sea to Europe.

A blanket manufacturer in a Tripoli suq operates the machinery used to weave the heavy yarn.

Small handicraft industries employed carpet weavers, metalsmiths, and leather workers. With the money earned from oil exports, Libya planned to greatly diversify its industries. By the 1980s, Libyan workers were producing machinery, household appliances, fertilizers, and industrial chemicals such as ammonium. Factories were also making steel pipes, drums, and other equipment for the oil-drilling industry.

Libya has successfully built up a new manufacturing sector, but these businesses are still closely tied to oil. When oil income declines because of falling prices, less money is available to import the raw materials needed for factories. A shortage of labor also sometimes slows or halts production at the largest factories. An embargo (ban) on trade imposed by the UN is also hurting Libyan businesses that are unable to sell their goods abroad.

By 1990 Libyan manufacturing was employing about 10 percent of the workforce and was contributing about half of the nation's gross national product (GNP)— the total value of all goods and services produced in a year. The most important manufactured products were cement, foodstuffs, refined petroleum, cigarettes, and industrial chemicals. Libyan factories also make clothing, leather goods, textiles, and shoes.

A worker packages jars of jam, a product that uses the harvest from Libya's fruit orchards.

Since the 1960s, the export of oil has been Libya's principal product of foreign trade. Oil has provided the country with a large trade surplus, meaning the country earns more from the sale of its exports than it spends on foreign imports. Oil makes up more than 95 percent of all Libyan exports, but Libya also sells animal hides and food. The most important buyers of Libyan oil are Italy, Spain, and Germany. Libya purchases machinery, cars, basic manufactured goods, transportation equipment, consumer goods, and food, mainly from Italy, France, Germany, and Japan.

Foreign investment historically has been important to the Libyan economy. European nations, including Britain and Italy, built the country's first manufacturing enterprises, and foreign oil companies developed Libya's oil drilling, shipping, and refining facilities. But poor relations with much of the outside world have discouraged new foreign investment. In addition, the threat of further UN trade sanctions against Libya, potentially to include a ban on oil exports, makes the country's economic future uncertain. Libya has

also reduced its own investments in foreign companies, fearing seizure of Libyan money and properties by foreign governments.

Agriculture and Fishing

Once largely agricultural, Libya still depends on limited fertile land to provide its people with food. The oil boom and the rise of industries drew many farmers into Libya's cities during the 1960s and 1970s. As a result, food production decreased, and the country had to depend increasingly on imports. About 18 percent of Libyans work in agriculture.

To combat the drop in food production, the government planned an ambitious irrigation program. Huge pipelines would bring water from underground aquifers in the Sahara to infertile tracts near the coast, where the government would set up self-sufficient, state-owned farms to be managed by committees of farmers. Because of this project, new pipelines are drying up wells that people in Saharan oases depend on to survive. Despite the program's goals, only about 1 percent of the land was under cultivation and only 8 percent was being used for pasture in the mid-1990s.

The most important agricultural regions in Libya are the Gefara Plain west of Tripoli and the Jabal al-Akhdar near Benghazi. Barley and wheat are the principal cereal crops, while millet is planted in Fezzan. Olive groves cover parts of the Gefara Plain and the Jabal Nafusah. Libyan farmers also harvest almonds, dates, onions, potatoes, and tobacco.

The raising of livestock, which traditionally has been an economically impor-

tant agricultural activity in Libya, centers mainly on sheep, goats, cattle, camels, and poultry. Sheep, which make up the largest and most productive herds, supply meat, milk, and wool. Although food production rose steadily in the early 1990s, Libya still depends on imports for about two-thirds of its food.

A small fishing fleet operates out of the port of Tripoli and along the country's northwestern coast. Fishing boats haul in tuna, sardines, and mullet for a small domestic market. Libya has granted Greek

Vendors in Libya unload crates of produce to sell at an open-air market. With very little domestic agriculture, Libya must import about 70 percent of its food supply.

Photo by Dick Bancroft

A young Libyan helps repair fishing nets along the coast outside Tripoli. The waters off Libya's Mediterranean coast are not highly productive, and only a tiny fraction of the workforce is employed in fishing.

fishing companies control of underwater sponge harvesting.

Transportation

Libyans have about 15,000 miles of roads, two-thirds of which are paved. The busiest route is a coastal highway that skirts the shores of the Mediterranean Sea from Tunisia east to Egypt. Other highways extend from this route southward to the oases of Sabha and Kufra. Public buses run between cities and towns, providing the most important means of transportation in Libya. Only one in ten Libyans owns an automobile. Although cars can survive desert travel, many desert dwellers depend on the hardy camel to cross the hot and waterless Saharan spaces.

Although Libya has no finished railways, the government is planning new lines that will link Misratah with Tripoli and a rail system at the Tunisian border. Another railroad may eventually be built to transport iron ore from Sabha in the Sahara to Misratah on the coast. Con-

Photo by Dick Bancroft

Although Libya lacks efficient roads through the Sahara, the highways along the coastline are modern and well traveled.

Construction workers raise a new building in Tripoli. Although Libya has experienced some slowdowns in economic growth, the country still benefits from a profitable oil industry. The government uses its substantial oil income to improve housing as well as to expand education, health care, and social services.

struction of a railroad between Benghazi and Egypt began in 1993.

Libya's largest and busiest port is Tripoli, which accommodates cargo ships as well as passenger ferries that sail to the Mediterranean island of Malta. Both Tripoli and Benghazi handle commercial shipments of heavy equipment and raw materials. Mersa Brega, a terminal point for several large pipelines, is the biggest of five ports used for the shipment of refined oil.

Libya has four large commercial airports—at Tripoli, Benghazi, Sabha, and Misratah. The state operates Jamahiriya Libyan Arab Airlines as the national carrier. But since April 1992, UN sanctions have ended commercial passenger traffic between Libya and the rest of the world.

The Future

By the mid-1990s, many Libyans were enjoying a much higher standard of living than had previous generations. The nation has left behind the poverty, hunger, and underdevelopment that it suffered through much of the twentieth century. Housing,

New European-style houses reflect the tastes of Libya's growing middle class. Some of these middle-class Libyans oppose the Qaddafi regime, wishing for more economic and personal freedoms in their country.

education, and health care have improved, and the country's economy is growing with revenues from oil production.

Libya's future prospects depend heavily on the oil market, which brings in most of the nation's export income. Although the government has tried to broaden the nation's industrial base, its efforts have been only partially successful. The revolutionary socialist government still discourages private and foreign investment. In addition, an uncertain political future makes foreign companies wary of making new investments in Libya.

In firm control of the country since 1969, the government of Muammar el-Qaddafi remains the single most important factor in Libya's future. To a great extent, Qaddafi's policies toward Libya's neighbors in North Africa and toward the rest of the world will decide the economic and social course Libya takes. The economy, for example, would benefit greatly if UN member nations traded with Libya.

Qaddafi, in turn, is greatly influenced by political conflicts in the Middle East, where many Arab governments are contending with revolutionary movements that Qaddafi supports. Despite Qaddafi's goal of a pan-Arab style of socialism, Libya still finds itself isolated among its many Arab neighbors.

Older Libyans *(left),* **many of whom remember and respect the traditions of Libya before the revolution, disagree with young Libyans** *(right)* **on the direction in which their nation should move, both politically and culturally.**

Libya's flag is entirely green, which is the official color of Islam.

Index